The Library of
NATIVE AMERICANS

The Shasta
of California and Oregon

Jack S. Williams

The Rosen Publishing Group's
PowerKids Press™
New York

For Jackie Stewart, my beloved sister and friend

Published in 2004 by The Rosen Publishing Group, Inc.
29 East 21st Street, New York, NY 10010

Photo and illustration credits: cover, pp. 18, 20, 21, 22, 25, 36, 38 Item # 6949, Neg # 32396, Cat No. 50/4067-4068-4069-4066, Item # 7010.jpg, Neg # 32394s, Neg # 32393, Neg # 32395, Neg # 32391, American Museum of Natural History Library; pp. 6, 9, 13 courtesy of the C. Hart Merriam Collection of Native American Photographs, The Bancroft Library, University of California, Berkeley; p. 7 © Morton Beebe/Corbis; p. 10 © David Muench/Corbis; p. 17 from "The Shasta" by Roland B. Dixon, in Bulletin of the American Museum of Natural History, Vol. XVII, Part V, July 1907, p. 394; pp. 20, 33, 40, 56 Courtesy of the Phoebe Apperson Hearst Museum of Anthropology and the Regents of the University of California, photographed by Eugene Golomshtok, Unit-ID: 15-6934, Unit-ID: 15-7540, Unit-ID: 15-7537; p. 24 National Anthropological Archives, Smithsonian Institution, Catalog No. 204258, 19286, 19282; p. 28 photo courtesy of Siskiyou County Museum, Yreka, California; p. 35 © Natalie Fobes/ Corbis; p. 42 reproduction of a painting by Cal Peters, courtesy of Tumacacori National Historic Park; p. 44 courtesy of the Seaver Center for Western History Research, Natural History Museum of Los Angeles; p. 46 © Hulton/Archive/Getty Images; p. 47 Library of Congress Geography and Map Division, Washington, D.C.; p. 48 Historic American Building Survey, Library of Congress, Prints and Photography Division, Washington, D.C.; p. 49 courtesy of the California History Room, California State Library, Sacramento, California.; p. 51 from *Pioneer Forts of the West*, Herbert M. Hart, Seattle, Superior Publishing Co., 1968, p. 120; p. 54 AP Photo/*San Francisco Examiner*, Kim Komenich; p. 57 AP Photo/Bob Galbraith.

Book Design: Erica Clendening

Williams, Jack S.
The Shasta of California and Oregon/ Jack S. Williams.— 1st ed.
    p. cm. — (Library of Native Americans)
Summary: Describes the history, culture, arts, government, and social structure of the Shasta people of California and Oregon, and gives a glimpse of Shasta life today.
Includes bibliographical references and index.
ISBN 1-4042-2663-X (lib. bdg.)
1. Shasta Indians—History—Juvenile literature. 2. Shasta Indians—Social life and customs—Juvenile literature. [1. Shasta Indians. 2. Indians of North America—California.] I. Title. II. Series.
E99.S33W55 2004
979.4004'9757—dc22
                                                                    2003014610

On the cover: A Shasta pine nut necklace.

A variety of terminologies has been employed in works about Native Americans. There are sometimes differences between the original names or terms used by a Native American group and the anglicized or modernized versions of such names or terms. Although this book contains terms that we feel will be most recognizable to our readership, there may also exist synonymous or native words that are preferred by certain speakers.

Contents

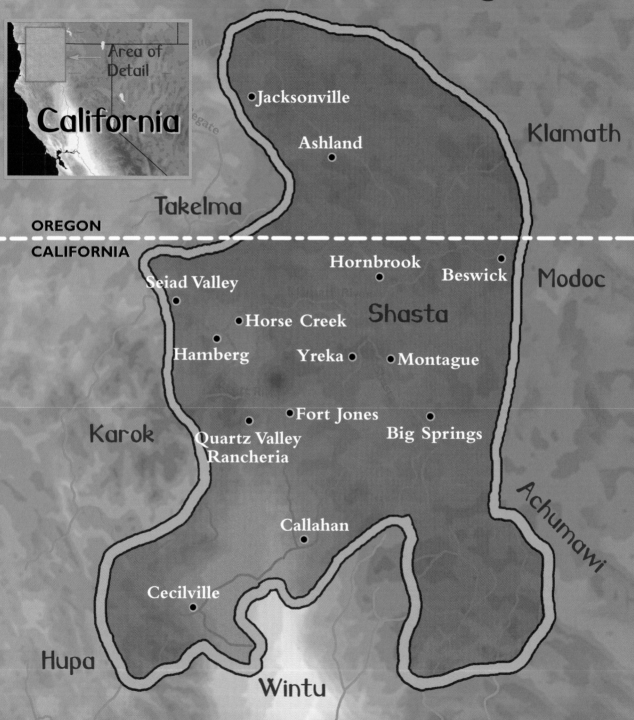

The Shasta and Their Neighbors

Area of
Detail

California

Jacksonville

Ashland

Klamath

Takelma

OREGON

CALIFORNIA

Hornbrook

Beswick

Modoc

Seiad Valley

Horse Creek

Shasta

Hamberg

Yreka

Montague

Karok

Fort Jones

Quartz Valley
Rancheria

Big Springs

Achumawi

Callahan

Cecilville

Hupa

Wintu

One

Introducing the Shasta People

Deep in the interior of northern California, far away from the coastline, there is an ancient land of fire and ice. This territory along the modern border with Oregon has many rugged mountains. Hanging in the heavens, high above the other peaks, Mount Shasta climbs an incredible 14,162 feet (4,316 meters) into the sky. For tens of thousands of years, this volcano has remained silent. Its peak is covered with spectacular white ice fields, called glaciers, that never melt. Mount Shasta overlooks hundreds of square miles of forests, rushing rivers, meadows, and lakes. The Rogue, Shasta, Scott, and Klamath Rivers thunder down the hillsides as they begin their long journeys to the Pacific Ocean. The native people who lived on the northern side of this mountain are also called the Shasta. They gave their name to the volcano and to one of the region's most important rivers.

The territory of the Shasta Nation included large parts of what are today Jackson County, Oregon, and Siskiyou County, California. Ancient homes of the Shasta people stood where many modern towns can be found. These places include Jacksonville, Ashland, Horse Creek, Big Springs, Hamburg, and Yreka. The

This map details the range of the Shasta territory.

5

main body of the Shasta Nation was divided into groups who inhabited the Klamath, Scott, and Shasta River valleys. There were several peoples that lived close to the main Shasta group who spoke similar languages and lived a similar way of life. These nations include the Konomihu, the Okwanuchu, and the New River Shasta. Because the mountains made it difficult for a person

to go from one valley to the next, the Shasta people also used group names that identified their home valleys. They realized that they shared very similar languages and similar ways of doing things with some of their neighbors, but they did not have a name for this larger group. Today, scholars and Native Americans alike use the name Shasta for all these peoples.

No one is certain where the word "Shasta" came from. The Native Americans we call Shasta did not use

This is a portrait of Shasta chief Moffett Creek Jake and his wife, taken in 1919. Over the centuries, the Shasta culture would survive many challenges.

the term to identify themselves until recent times. Some people believe that it came from a Russian word. Eastern European settlers arrived in California in 1812 and built a fort on the coast at Bodega Bay. According to people who think that these settlers created the name, the Russian colonists eventually identified the great white mountain to their north as Tchastal. This means "white, or pure, mountain." The experts who believe this story think that people from the United States later changed the spelling to Shasta. The scholars in favor of a Russian origin of the word argue that it was later applied to the Native Americans who lived at the northern end of the mountain. Other researchers think the term came from the personal name of a native leader called Shastika. He lived in the region around 1850, when the first large groups of non–Native Americans moved into the Shasta region.

In 1812, Europeans settled the area known as Bodega Bay in California. The fort near Bodega Bay would allow for newcomers to move east and into the Shasta land.

Origins

The researchers who study where the earliest Americans came from cannot say exactly when the first Shasta people arrived in the region in what is now California. By studying the remains left behind by ancient peoples, archaeologists have developed an understanding of some of the things that happened. Most archaeologists think the distant ancestors of Native Americans came from Asia sometime between 13,000 and 40,000 years ago. These people arrived in North America by crossing over a series of bridges that were made of ice and land. These frozen surfaces connected a series of small islands that still exist in the northern part of the Pacific Ocean. The first people who crossed these land bridges lived by hunting. They moved to the east and south, following herds of grazing animals, such as caribou. As time passed, the hunters moved farther and farther south. Eventually, they reached the southern tip of South America.

Among the many waves of people that came from the north were the ancestors of the Shasta Nation. Many experts believe that the Hokan-speaking peoples, who included the Shasta, were the first human beings to permanently settle in present-day California. The study of ancient languages suggests that the entire state of California was covered by Hokan speakers by 4000 BC. All of the native groups who came from other language families, such as the Penutian speakers, the Shoshone speakers, and the Athabascan speakers, arrived at a later time. These more recent arrivals formed nations that occupied the lands that surrounded the Hokan-speaking Shasta peoples. Nearly all of these movements of people took place by AD 1000.

This is a 1918 photograph of Klamath Canyon, an important part of the Shasta territory. The Shasta world was rich in diverse plant and animal life.

9

Two
Daily Life

When the first non–Native Americans reached the Shasta region, they found a people who lived in a close relationship with nature. While few of the newcomers appreciated it, the Shasta people had achieved a remarkable ability to use the natural world that surrounded them. Their amazing way of life is still the focus of many researchers who believe that there are important lessons that we can learn from the Shasta Nation.

Living in a Mountain World

The Shasta people live in a mountainous region. All of their country stands at elevations above 2,500 feet (762 m). This territory supported all the food, water, and other natural resources that they required. However, it took hard work to gather these treasures from the land. Life was beautiful in the shadow of Mount Shasta, but it was also difficult. The surrounding forests were home to elk, antelope, deer, bears, raccoons, coyotes, and many other large animals. The lakes and streams had dozens of kinds of fish, including magnificent salmon and trout, and waterfowl, such as ducks. Like nearly all other Native Americans, these people also had dogs that helped in hunting and lived as family pets.

The mighty Mount Shasta was a magnificent feature of the Shasta world. Mount Shasta stands at nearly 14,162 feet (4,316 m) above sea level.

The plant life of the Shasta region was also very rich. The hills had pine and oak forests. The nuts from these trees were important food sources for the Native Americans. There were also manzanita berries, wild plums, wild grapes, chokecherries, milkweed, and dozens of other kinds of plants with tasty seeds or roots. The lakeshores produced other useful plants, including reeds and edible bulbs.

The Shasta people did not have farms. However, they did work hard to encourage the growth of certain kinds of plants, such as grasses and oak trees, by setting fires that would burn away unwanted plants. The scorched land would allow for wanted plants to move in and thrive. They would also scatter seeds to increase the harvests of the plants they liked or needed. During the dry months, baskets of water were poured onto the most delicate plants that might otherwise shrivel and die.

Each year, the seasons brought a cycle of change and rebirth to the land. The warm days of spring gave way to the heat of summer. Fall brought with it a time when many wild plants were harvested. The winters were very cold. Snow covered the ground, and ice formed on many of the watery surfaces.

Each of the seasons and the many forms of life had a place in the Shasta world. Most of the Shasta people spent the five worst months of winter in their main villages. These settlements were found at lower elevations along the main waterways. The winter villages were located at the warmest places. During the summer, the Shasta people moved into the higher areas in order to take advantage of the food and other resources that grew there during this season. Whatever time of year it was, the Shasta people remained busy. The women and children were usually the ones who gathered wild plants while the adult males did most of the hunting.

Villages

The Shasta people lived in villages. The abundance of food and other resources made it possible for many of them to live all year in a relatively

Because of the changing climate, most Shasta moved from houses in the mountains to those in the valleys, depending on the season. This house was built by the Wintu, a Shasta neighbor. The Shasta built similar structures.

small area. The number of people who lived in a village depended on the resources that were available. Some communities had as many as fifty people. Other villages included only a single family.

There were probably 150 Shasta villages by 1800. Most of the settlements in the Klamath Valley were built at a place where a stream entered into the river. In other areas of the Shasta territory, villages were found where streams dropped into the valleys. A small number of settlements were built away from the rivers, near major oak forests.

Most of the Shasta people used two kinds of houses. During the winter, each family built a rectangular home that measured about sixteen by twenty feet (5 by 6 m). These structures were called umma. The walls and roofs were created using dirt and wood. Much of the wood was shaped into rough planks of unequal lengths. The structure was assembled inside a pit that measured between three and six feet (1 and 2 m) deep. The roof had steeply sloping sides that dropped in two directions. The top of the structure had a small opening that allowed smoke to escape and made it possible for sunlight to enter the room. The entrances to the houses usually faced the water. A single opening was created at one end of the rectangle. A door was made from hide or reeds. The center of the room had a fire pit. Men and women worked together to create the winter houses during the early summer.

During the spring, most of the Shasta people moved into villages in the high country. Their temporary mountain homes were brush or bark huts. Older people and individuals who were not strong enough to climb into the mountainous places stayed home. They took care of the main village while their relatives were away. Most of the summer houses were round and less than ten feet (3 m) in diameter. The walls formed small domes or cones. In the Shasta Valley, the people lived in larger cone-shaped houses that were similar to their winter homes. Several families would share one large structure.

The furniture in the houses included wooden stools, reed mats, and bundles of reeds that served as a carpet. The plant coverings were used as beds. In some of the Shasta territory, pine needles replaced reeds. The sheets and covers were made from reeds and animal skins, such as deer hide, elk hide, and even imported bison hide. The cooking tools were kept in two areas near the door. The walls were lined with the family possessions. Much of the space was taken up by storage baskets and reed sacks that were filled with dried fish, dried meat, and edible plants that had been ground into flour.

The larger villages had assembly halls called okwa-umma. These larger structures were used as gathering places for the village. Inside the assembly hall, community members would meet and make decisions and hold special celebrations. Sometimes large groups of visitors would be allowed to sleep in the halls. A few Shasta settlements also used their community buildings for sweat houses or as multi-family homes. The assembly halls were usually found at the middle of the village. The chiefs were usually placed in charge of the structure's construction and plan. Their sons inherited the ownership of the structure. If there was no male to inherit the building, it was abandoned.

Some of the larger Shasta villages also had sweat houses. These buildings were called wukwu. They were similar to assembly houses, except that they were smaller in size. Only men and boys were allowed inside. The larger wukwus could hold up to twenty people. When they could, men often worked all day inside these structures. When a boy reached the age of ten or twelve, he moved into the sweat house and slept there until he married. The men and boys kept a small fire glowing at the center of the room. When they decided to have a sweat bath, fuel was added to the fire, and the room was filled with hot air and smoke. After a period of time inside the sweat house, the males would take a bath in a nearby body of water. People took sweat baths for fun, for religious purposes, and as part of healing ceremonies. Sometimes the men took sweat baths before they went hunting. The night before they left, the hunters burned strong-smelling plants, such as sage. This would mask the hunter's natural scent, making it easier to sneak up on prey such as deer and elk.

Every village also had an area set aside for storing food, such as acorns and dried meat. Each family would dig a pit and line the walls with leaves or reeds. Once the pit was filled, the contents were covered with leaves, or reeds, and dirt.

Every village had its own cemetery. Each family owned an area where it buried the remains of its dead relatives. After someone died, his or her house was torn down or burned, and his or her family would have to build a new one.

Cooking

Among the Shasta people, women usually prepared food. They used many different methods to create a wide variety of delicious meals. The Shasta dishes reflected the abundant sources of nourishment that could be found in the natural world that surrounded them.

In order to transform wild foods into flour, the Shasta people used large flat rocks and cylinder-shaped stones called pestles. A special kind of basket that had no bottom was used to keep the flour from blowing away. When these three components were used together they were called a hopper mortar. The nuts of pine trees and oaks

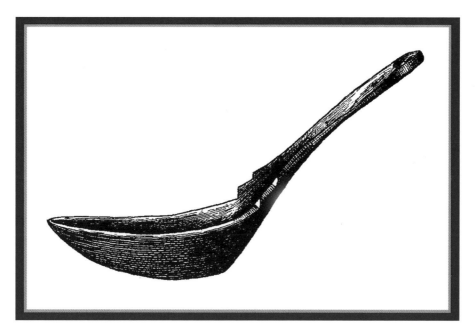

Wooden spoons, similar to the one in this illustration, were made by skilled Shasta craftspeople.

were probably the most important kinds of ground foods that the Shasta peoples ate. Acorns were ground into powder and then soaked in water to eliminate the natural poisons that they contained. The grinding tools could also be used to tenderize tough meat.

Dried fish, fish bones, and dried meat were also ground into flour. This powder could later be combined with water to create a nutritious paste.

Many of the different types of food were heated or roasted over an open flame. Meat and fish were often smoked. The Shasta cooks used tightly woven baskets to prepare liquids. The woven containers were filled with the ingredients of the meals and small stones that had been heated in a fire. The mixture had to be constantly stirred, or the stones would burn a hole in the basket. Using similar techniques, the Shasta peoples toasted insects, such as crickets and

This Shasta rattle *(left)* and meat brush were made from deer parts. After hunting the Shasta used nearly every part of the animal.

grasshoppers. A relatively small number of people had stone bowls that were used to heat liquids. Acorn flour and similar kinds of flour were mixed with water to form dough. Small cookie-like loafs were baked on hot rocks next to a fire.

Some Shasta cooks also used earthen ovens or pits to roast food. The first thing that the women would do is dig a deep hole. Then they would build a fire in the pit. The fire would be allowed to burn for several hours before the glowing embers would be removed using sticks. The food was wrapped and tied in leaves and placed in the hole. Dirt or rocks were then piled on top of the food. A few hours later, the cooks would dig out the roasted bundles. When the packets were opened, their ingredients were ready to eat. Roasting pits were also used to get pinecones to open up and release their nuts.

Many of the Shasta foods, such as wild berries, could be eaten without any preparation. Milkweed was chewed like bubble gum. Manzanita berries were crushed and combined with water to make a delicious ciderlike drink.

Most of the Shasta people ate two meals each day. When guests dropped in, they were always served a special meal. Everyone had their own serving basket, which they used at mealtime.

Clothing and Body Decoration

The Shasta people wore a variety of different types of basic clothing. These items generally reflected the cold climate that they lived in.

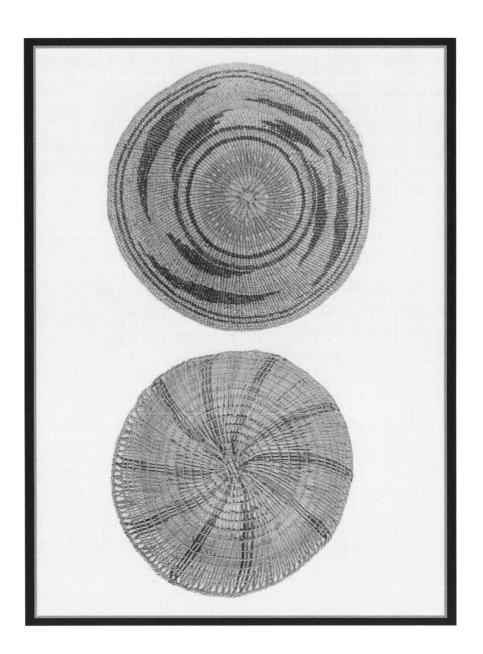

Woven baskets like these were an important part of Shasta culture.

Most men and women wore shirts, small caps, and many different kinds of belts. The men used leggings. Women usually wore skirts and aprons. Heavier robes, blankets, and capes were also worn, especially during the winter months. Other special cold-weather gear included fur hats and fur leggings. Everyone wore moccasins. These ranged in size from ankle height to waist height, depending on the group and weather. Some of the Shasta people also made slipper-like shoes out of reeds. When snow filled the landscape, men and women also wore kite-shaped snowshoes. Many of the skin garments had fringes. Some items were covered with beadwork.

Each of the major groups of the Shasta people had their own hairstyles. Most of the men wore their hair long. It was sometimes allowed to fall over the shoulders. Other men wore their hair put up in the back with a pin. The men and women changed the details of their styles as they grew older. Everyone wore jewelry that included beads and pendants made from seashells, pine nuts, elk teeth, bear claws and

This skirt was worn by a Shasta woman. It was made out of coarse grasses and reeds.

teeth, and feathers. Both men and women pierced their ears and noses in order to wear special jewelry. Other body decorations included tattoos. The adult women had three wide stripes tattooed on their chins.

When a Shasta baby was only a few days old, its mother tied its head down to a flat wooden cradle board. This caused the shape of the skull to change. The flat-headed look was considered to be very beautiful to the Shasta. This kind of change, called cranial deformation, also helped the Shasta people to recognize other members of their nation. Similar methods were used by many different groups all over the world to make them look more attractive.

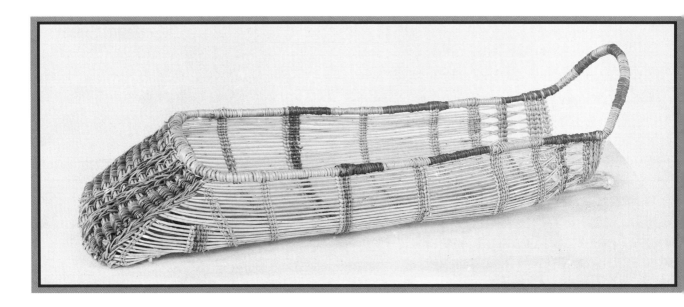

Made from reed and straw, this carrier was used to transport babies of Shasta women.

On special occasions, such as ceremonies, community leaders wore feather collars and headdresses. Many of these coverings incorporated brightly colored woodpecker scalps. The women often wore feathers in their hair. During rituals, red, white, yellow, and black body paint was sometimes worn. Ceremonial clothing was often covered with beadwork and decorations made using porcupine quills.

Arts and Crafts

The Shasta people made amazingly beautiful and practical objects. They created nearly all these items from the natural resources that they found near their homes.

The Native American men were experts at making tools out of stones. Obsidian (which is an especially sharp kind of volcanic glass), flint, basalt, and similar rocks were collected to create chipped-stone implements. These objects included drills, arrowheads, spearheads, knives, and scrapers. Other rocks, like granite and sandstone, were ground to create pestles. The Shasta people also pounded and scraped soapstone to make bowls and the ends of wooden smoking pipes. Unlike objects made from other rocks, the soapstone products did not crack or break apart when they were heated in a fire.

Much of the mountainous Shasta region did not have a plentiful supply of the special kinds of tree shoots, rushes, reeds, and

grasses that were favored by basket makers. As a result, the Shasta people acquired many of these items through trade with their neighbors. Despite the shortage in raw materials, the region's women still created several basic varieties of baskets, including jars, bowls, trays, fans, and boxes. The raw materials were woven together using many different patterns. By changing the materials while making the baskets, the craftswomen could create many interesting designs.

The plant world was a source of many other raw materials that were important in everyday life. Wood was an essential fuel for fire used to cook and heat. Every family needed a lot of fuel, especially during the cold winter months. Wood was also turned into smoking pipes, digging sticks, poles for harvesting acorns and pinecones, arrow shafts, spears,

24 These bowls demonstrate the skill of the Shasta craftspeople. Bowls made by the Shasta were practical as well as beautiful.

The Shasta made many things that helped them adapt to the land they lived in. They crafted snowshoes, like the one pictured here, to help them hunt and travel in the sometimes difficult mountain terrain.

spoons, bowls, cups, house poles, stirring paddles, and trays. The sap from pine trees produced an excellent glue. Wild hemp fibers were woven to produce strong threads or cords. In the northern Shasta area, the people who lived near larger bodies of water used canoes made by burning and carving out the center of a large tree, such as a sugar pine. In the south, the Shasta people made canoe-shaped rafts out of reeds. These boats were made by tying bundles of reeds together. Both kinds of vessels could hold one or two people.

The Shasta hunters and warriors made powerful bows from a combination of wood and deer tendon, called sinew. These bows were carefully painted with designs that the Shasta believed would help their arrows find their targets. The arrows were painted with similar patterns, allowing each of the archers to identify his missiles.

The animal world also provided other important resources to the Shasta people. Skins, sinew, and fur were made into clothing, bags, drums, and blankets. Deer hooves became rattles and pendants. Animal and human hair was used to make thread and cords. Animal bones and horns were turned into hairpins, scrapers, fishhooks, awls, needles, jewelry, game equipment, and combs. Elk kneecaps and deer skulls proved to be especially useful for spoons, and some of the larger bones were used like hammers. Shasta villagers used bird feathers to make arrows, special headdresses, some kinds of clothing, and decorations used in rituals. Fish provided an important kind of glue.

Trade

The Shasta people were excellent traders. A number of things were acquired from other groups. Baskets were collected from nearly all of the Shasta's neighbors. Salt, seaweed, shells, beads, and otter skins were gathered by people who lived along the coast. Obsidian that was used to make sharp, chipped stone tools was obtained from the neighboring Achumawi people. Canoes and pine nut necklaces were created by the Wintu, who lived south of the Shasta. Even bison skins came to California from the faraway plains in the east. The Shasta people offered many different kinds of goods in trades. These included buckskins, pine nuts, stone tools, wolf skins, woodpecker scalps, acorn flour, ground dried salmon, and juniper beads made from juniper berries.

The Shasta people also traded resources and goods within their territory. When a group from one valley went to visit with another, they often brought food, which was exchanged for local products. The Shasta also went on trips to neighboring villages in order to gamble. These exchanges also provided a kind of trade between settlements.

For many kinds of basic commerce, the Shasta people used shell beads as money. Almost everything, including people, was assigned a certain number of beads. If a person died in an accident or as a result of a crime, the chiefs would try to get the people who were responsible to pay the surviving family members whatever amount the person was worth.

Three

Other Aspects of Shasta Life

Village life among the Shasta was broken into many groups. A person was assigned to a group on the basis of where he or she lived, his or her gender, his or her wealth, his or her age, and who his or her relatives were.

The Shasta people's smallest social group was the family. If a man wanted to get married, he had to give the wife's family a certain amount of money. Most of the time, people from the same village did not get married. An unmarried couple usually moved in with the husband's relatives. When a man died, his oldest brother or son inherited his property, including the rights to use certain fishing or hunting areas. Some families owned better locations than others. These people had more possessions and could have been considered wealthy.

One or more families formed a village. The leaders of the village included chiefs and the older people, who formed a council of advisors. The Shasta people also had a number of doctors and religious leaders. These groups owned sacred objects that were thought to hold special powers. The doctors and religious leaders were always treated with respect. Sometimes, people feared them because they were scared that the doctors would use their powers to hurt them. Most of the doctors were women.

This photograph shows a Shasta named Sargent Sambo wearing traditional clothing around the turn of the twentieth century. Sargent Sambo was one of the last hereditary chiefs of the Shasta people.

Several villages found in the same river valley formed a larger community. This group was headed by the most influential chief. All the Shasta people, including the men who dominated the valleys, recognized a common connection through the regional chief who lived on the Rogue River. However, before the modern era, the Shasta people did not think of themselves as a nation with a defined overall government. They were, first and foremost, members of a family and members of an individual village.

None of the leaders outside of an individual's family could directly order them to do something. Beyond the family, the natives had a great deal of freedom to choose if they were going to go along with the wishes of their political leaders. Although a few people had more things or greater influence, most of the Shasta people thought of themselves as equals.

Government

Every Shasta person belonged to a particular village. The people of each village owed their political loyalty to their village leader or chief. This man was expected to settle the disputes that took place between families. The chiefs also provided leadership when there was a crisis. However, the chiefs were rarely the ones who were placed in charge during a war. Village leaders were usually assisted by a council made up of elders. There was also a special chief for each of the four major regional divisions of the Shasta people, including the Shasta Valley, the Rogue River Valley, the Klamath Valley, and the New River Shasta area. The Rogue River leader, who lived in a region that would eventually become part of Oregon, was the person to whom the others turned when they faced problems that they could not agree on. Each of the chiefs inherited his office from his older brother or his father. Sometimes Shasta people would form a temporary alliance with other Native American communities. However, these agreements always ended once a war or a similar crisis had come to an end.

The people of the village had to give special gifts of food and other things to their chief. Although they were given respect, the village leaders were limited in what they could order people to do. When someone in his area committed a crime, the village leader would often arrange for the person who had done something wrong to pay a fine to the victim. If the individual who had committed the crime could not pay, the chief used his own money. The people who were victims were required to accept the payments, but were sometimes also allowed to take direct action against the criminal as an additional form of justice. The chiefs also shared their food and other possessions when there were shortages.

Every chief was also required to give speeches in order to convince his followers to be kind, to keep peace with their neighbors, and to work hard. A village leader's wife often gave similar presentations to the women of the community. Most chiefs tried to get people to do what was right by setting an example.

Warfare

The Shasta people usually tried to avoid wars. However, fights did sometimes break out between rival villages and alliances. There were many causes of these struggles. Sometimes the war started when a person from one community killed someone from another. On other occasions, communities went to war when they feared that a religious leader from another settlement was using supernatural powers against them. Some warriors wanted war so that they could become wealthy or gain prestige. When they were fighting with non-Shasta peoples, the war parties tried to capture women. Their relatives would have to pay their captors to get them back. The Shasta Valley people also captured enemy children, who they turned into slaves.

The Shasta peoples fought many wars with their neighbors, including the Modoc and the Wintu. The Modoc often attacked the Shasta region during the summer. As a result, the Klamath Valley and Shasta Valley people joined forces. They often entered Modoc territory with a similar objective of killing and stealing.

There were also many conflicts fought between the regional communities that made up the Shasta Nation. The Shasta Valley and Scott Valley groups were often at war with each other, and there were also conflicts between the Klamath River Shasta and the Kammatwa.

The main Shasta weapons consisted of bows and arrows and spears. In order to protect themselves in combat, some of the warriors wore a kind of armor made from elk hide and wooden rods. The rods, made of split branches, were held together by hemp cords. The armor

Arrow shaft straighteners, such as the one pictured above, were extremely useful tools for the Shasta.

protected the wearer's chest and back. The warriors sometimes painted black and red geometric designs on their breastplates. Many men also wore a protective headband of hide. This headgear served as a helmet. When they expected to fight, the Shasta warriors often wore war paint, covering their faces and other areas of exposed skin with painted circular spots. These helped identify friends and allies, as well as acted as religious symbols.

When a war party was created, those who decided to fight elected the person who would be in charge. They usually selected the most experienced or most skilled warrior. The men and women of the village would gather and hold a special ritual and dance that were designed to make the members of the war party more courageous. When the men returned, they often held a similar victory dance as a celebration.

Sometimes small armies of warriors would come together and fight regular battles. In other conflicts, the two sides would ambush each other, or run sneak attacks. Other times they would simply attempt to steal things from their enemies. Much of the fighting took place at night. Sometimes women and older girls joined military expeditions. Shasta elders reported that when they saw the enemy, they would rush forward with sharp knives in order to cut their enemies bowstrings and quivers. The women probably also carried military equipment, helped out with captives, and carried whatever was taken from raiding their enemy.

Occasionally, during conflicts, one side sent out messengers to arrange some kind of peaceful settlement. In order to avoid more bloodshed, the group that wanted peace would pay the other side a special fee and hold a peace ceremony. Both war parties would meet at a prearranged place during the daytime. There, the warriors danced with their weapons and armor before they disarmed and went home.

Hunting and Fishing

The Shasta were famous hunters and fishermen. Before they went out, the participants often burned small offerings of tobacco or

Salmon were a very abundant and important food resource in the mountainous Shasta region.

similar plants. This was done in order to gain the help of supernatural forces. Many communities began their hunts with other rituals. These celebrations included dances, singing, and prayers. While they were hunting, the men had to follow many other religious rules. The rules showed respect for the animal and natural world. It was not enough to simply kill the creature and bring it home to be used as food.

36   This bird feather wand *(above)* and skunk pelt are examples of objects the Shasta made following the hunts.

The hunters used many different techniques to capture and kill the creatures that they hunted. The main weapon that they relied on was the powerful Shasta bow and arrow. Sometimes a team of men would drive animals into a brush enclosure to trap them. Fire could also be used to force a larger animal, such as a deer or bear, into a place where it could be killed. Some hunters drove creatures into large pits. Others set up traps equipped with giant rocks that could fall onto the animals. Basket traps or snares were often used to capture birds and other small creatures. Dogs often played an important part in chasing the prey.

Both the men and women fished. As with hunting, there were many rituals that had to be observed. The salmon and other fish were sacred creatures. They were captured using many techniques. Sometimes several families would work together to create giant systems of nets that spanned a river or stream. The Shasta people also relied on many other fishing devices, including nets, special baskets, stone fish traps, hooks and lines, spears, and harpoons.

Religion and Community Gatherings

The Shasta people had many interesting ideas about religion. There were special rituals held when people became doctors, when children reached the age of thirteen, and when warriors went off to battle. A great deal of the Shasta's religion involved rituals that the families performed in private or when a person was alone. Through right actions, the Shasta people had to work hard to balance the forces in the world that surrounded them.

Religious celebrations marked each stage of a person's life. There were many rules about what a person could eat and the places where he or she could go. Some activities required ritual visits to the

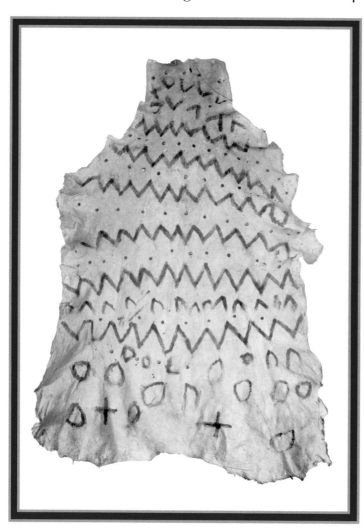

sweat houses. The ritual dances usually included music that was performed using hide drums, rattles made from deer hooves, and bone and wood flutes.

The Shasta elders taught the young people many different religious stories. For example, some stories told of why people wore charcoal on their faces after someone had died. They said that after the death of the child of Black Cricket, the very first creature that died,

This Shasta shirt made from animal hide was used in religious ceremonies. The Shasta used almost every part of the animals they hunted and killed.

Coyote, who was another supernatural being, had prevented the child from being brought back to life. Black Cricket then buried the child. Since that time, people who were sad because someone they knew had died, covered their faces with pitch and charcoal, so that they would look like Black Cricket. When a story lesson was over, the young people tried to repeat it using the same words as their teachers. This way, the stories were told over and over again for centuries, with very few changes.

When a young boy reached the age of thirteen, he was expected to go off into the high mountains in search of a vision that would improve his ability to hunt, fish, or gamble. The vision usually came in the form of a special dream. Some men repeated this journey several times during their lives. The most important ceremony for girls also took place when they reached age thirteen. The girl who was celebrating the event had to spend a great deal of time away from the village. During this period, she was taught special rituals.

Elaborate ceremonies also marked many other occasions in an adult's life. There were special prayers, rituals, and dances for marriages and births and for when a person took on special responsibilities as a leader, warrior, or doctor.

When a Shasta villager died, he or she was usually buried in the community cemetery. If he or she died far away from home, his or her remains could be cremated, or burned to ash. His or her ashes would then be brought to the village for burial. A dead person's property was burned or buried with him or her during the funeral.

40   Religious ceremonies were very important to the Shasta culture. The first salmon catch each year was honored by the Shasta. The Shasta did not eat any of their salmon catch until after the nearby Karuk performed the White Deerskin Dance *(shown above)*.

Many of the religious beliefs of the Shasta people involved health. Their doctors had to understand numerous powerful supernatural energies. People often grew sick after they met one of these forces. The sickness could cause death if they did not receive proper treatment. The methods used by the doctors involved prayers and special rituals, as well as the patient avoiding certain activities and foods. The doctors were usually paid for their work.

Four

Dealing with the Newcomers

The first Spanish explorers reached what is now California in 1540. During the 200 years that followed, there were many other European visitors. However, none of these explorers and settlers reached the interior of northern California, where the Shasta people made their homes.

Despite the fact that the Shasta people never saw the foreigners, they did suffer many problems as a result of their arrival. Although they did not intend to, the Europeans brought terrible diseases that spread from native nation to native nation. Illnesses like smallpox and measles killed hundreds of thousands of people throughout North America. We do not have any written records of the era in northern California. However, based on what happened in other areas, it is likely that the population of the Shasta people was greatly reduced during this era. One expert estimated the loss at nearly a third of the total population. By the time explorers reached the Shasta territory around 1850, its people had probably gone through a terrible decline followed by a slow recovery.

During the eighteenth century, Spanish soldiers and settlers explored and settled other parts of California, but left the Shasta region untouched.

The Shasta Peoples and Outsiders
1769–1850

Between 1769 and 1850, Spaniards, Mexicans, Russians, and Americans each claimed control of the land that would become California. Although the colonists of these nations existed in the area of California, the Shasta people lived in a region that these foreigners rarely visited.

Relations between Europeans and Native Americans were stressed, and oftentimes bloody, for more than 100 years. This illustration depicts a conflict between a Spanish soldier and Native Americans near Monterey, California, far south of the Shasta territory.

Most of the Spanish and Mexican colonists lived on the coast between San Francisco and San Diego. The Russians held a tiny portion of the coastline around Bodega Bay. These intruders never ventured into what would become the California-Oregon borderlands. Fur trappers, who included Americans and citizens of the British Empire, were the first outsiders to wander through the Shasta territory. Between 1820 and 1846, they passed through the country during their search for beaver pelts and other animal skins that could be sold at high prices in Asia and Europe. The foreigners came from settlements located on the coast of modern Washington and Oregon. The Shasta country did not include many of the animals that the trappers were interested in.

During this period, a particularly bad epidemic broke out among the Shasta people. The cause of the disease was unclear. It may have been malaria, a kind of disease spread by mosquitoes and introduced to North America by the Europeans. So many people died between 1830 and 1833 that the Shasta leaders tried to block the entrance of any non-native person into their communities.

By 1846, some of the outsiders' trade goods were beginning to become important to the Shasta people. Iron tools were extremely valuable for cutting wood and doing other similar tasks. However, very few of these precious items reached the Shasta region. Tobacco, which was smoked, was a luxury that could be grown. Shasta men soon grew their own small fields of the leafy plant. Undoubtedly, it was in this period that some Shasta craftspeople also began to use glass beads and steel needles. The items imported at this time included neither horses nor firearms.

45

The Gold Rush

It was not until 1848 that events were set in motion that would bring large numbers of newcomers into the Shasta world. The discovery of gold in the Sierra Nevada inspired exploration of other areas in California. In 1848, the precious metal was found

After the gold rush, parts of the landscape of the Shasta region were drastically changed. Mining towns would spring up seemingly overnight. The miners would take what they wanted and leave the rest, turning the land into a barren wasteland.

just south of the Shasta territory, at Readings Bar. Seemingly overnight, hordes of newcomers invaded the region. The stories of the miners' adventures are exciting. The colorful figures of the time include notorious gamblers and robbers, like Rattlesnake Dick. While some of these men found fortunes, the gold rush was usually not pleasant or fun. The arrival of the miners started an era of incredible suffering for the native people. For the Shasta Nation in particular, the presence of gold in their homeland spelled misfortune.

The search for gold brought large numbers of non–Native Americans into the Shasta territory. Most of the miners believed that all native people should either be killed, sent to some other place, or forced to change lifestyles to be more like Europeans. They soon began to slaughter the Shasta people. When white people arrived, they simply took over the native property, stealing the land and all that it contained. They justi-fied their actions by

During the late nineteenth century, more and more towns began to spring up in the Shasta region. This illustration, done in 1884, shows the early years of Yreka, California, under the shadow of Mount Shasta.

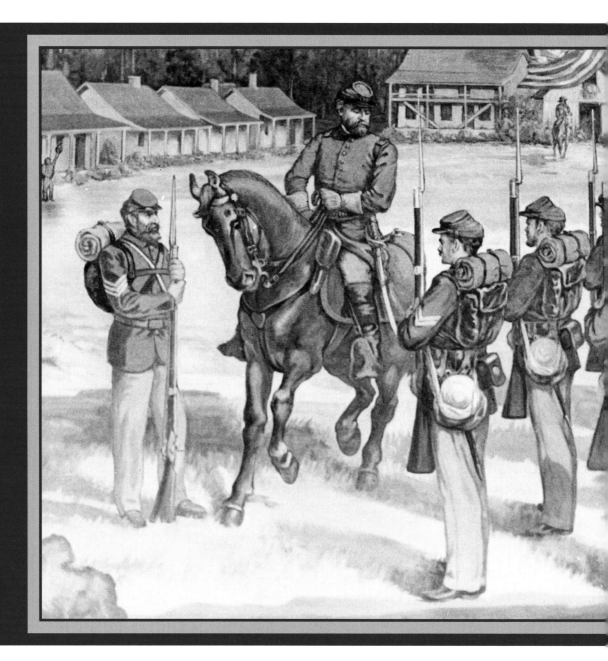

This painting *(left)* captures the scene at Fort Humboldt in northern California. American soldiers under government orders would play a key role in destroying the Shasta way of life. Governor Peter Burnett *(above)*, who took office in 1849, imposed many rules and restrictions that made life for the Shasta very difficult.

saying that the Shasta had no rights, since they were not really human beings.

In the state capital of Sacramento, California, Governor Peter H. Burnett and most of the legislature agreed with these horribly unfair policies. Governor Burnett stated that he looked forward to the complete destruction of every single native community in the state. Judges and courts encouraged the newcomers to enslave Native American children and force adults to do whatever they felt was in their interests. Not everyone agreed with Burnett's policies. Some people in the United States government tried to create a program that would allow mining that would also be fair to Native Americans.

On October 6, 1851, some of the Shasta people made a treaty with representatives of the United States. The Shasta people were to be given a portion of Scott Valley in exchange for giving up their claim to the rest of their homeland. The treaty appealed to some Native Americans because the government also promised to stop the miners from attacking their villages. Unfortunately, the U.S. Congress refused to ratify, or put into law, the treaty. Many non–Native Americans believed that the native peoples had been given too much. To the miners, the only acceptable solution was the death of every last Native American.

Fighting Back

Between 1853 and 1856, the Shasta people tried to protect themselves in what were called the Rogue River Wars. They were joined by members of many of the Native American nations that had been their traditional enemies. This struggle was a desperate attempt to survive. This conflict was more like a program of extermination than it was an actual war. During the fighting, the soldiers in blue from Fort Jones, Fort Lane, and Fort Humboldt helped informal bands of miners as they moved through the backcountry, killing any Native American they encountered. Some Shasta signed a treaty to end the

Built in 1852, Fort Jones would be abandoned by the U.S. Army by 1858. The fort would then become an active trading center in the Shasta territory.

first war in 1853. This event established a small reservation on the Rogue River at Table Rock. However, the miners' attacks continued. In 1855, a second war began. Some native warriors fought back. Many of the people who did not want to fight moved to Fort Lane, where they hoped that the army might be able to protect them. The native leaders could not figure out any way that they could win. There were just too many newcomers.

In 1856, the Rogue River Reservation was closed. The Shasta survivors who had fought on both sides of the California-Oregon border, as well as those who did not, were rounded up. The people were moved like cattle to a reservation at Grande Ronde and, later, to Fort Hoskins in Oregon, at the eastern entrance to the Siletz Indian Reservation. It was a shameful moment in American history.

By 1870, the traditional Shasta way of life had been nearly destroyed. Surviving Native Americans preserved as many traditions as they could. Many of the Shasta people joined the religious movement founded by Wovoka, a Shoshone living in Walker Pass in northeastern California. He had a vision that through special prayers and rituals, the newcomers would disappear and the stolen lands would be returned to their Native American owners. Unfortunately for native peoples, this movement failed to produce the restoration of their rights and property. Diseases, hopelessness, and poverty made the lives of the Shasta people miserable. Each year, there were fewer and fewer Native Americans.

One of the last traditional hereditary chiefs of all the Shasta people was known to the whites as Sargent Sambo. During the early twentieth century, he worked with many scholars to record various aspects of the Shasta way of life. He probably did more to record important information than any other individual during this difficult era.

By 1910, the Shasta population, which had once numbered about 6,000 people, had declined to fewer than 120 persons. In 1958, the last two Shasta reservations in California at Quartz Valley and Ruffeys were eliminated. The remaining lands were divided among the forty-two inhabitants. Henceforth, the state and federal government would no longer recognize the Shasta people as a legal Native American nation.

Five

The Shasta Today

All the terrible things that happened to the Shasta communities have made it hard for them to preserve their ancient ways. Still, these Native Americans have never given up. Today, there are about 1,200 people who recognize that they have Shasta ancestors. Many members of the surviving Shasta Nation disagree with the government's 1958 decision to eliminate the two remaining Shasta reservations. Since that time, the Shasta people have not received the same benefits of health care, lands, and other rights that are given to Native Americans who have reservations. They want to be recognized again as a Native American nation by the federal and state governments. The members of more than sixty other native groups in California are in a similar situation. Despite these circumstances, the Shasta people still want to take care of their ancient homeland. Many government and private organizations prevent them from going back to their ancient places and make it all but impossible for them to honor their ancestors or worship. Their sacred places are often overrun by tourists who disregard the natives' attempts to preserve them for the future.

In 1990, there were only twelve Shasta speakers alive, and none of these people lived in California. Four years later, one expert

Today, Shasta Dam at Shasta Lake supplies much of the region with energy. Mount Shasta can be seen in the background.

56 Over time, outsiders began to deny that any Shasta survived. This photograph, taken in 1926, shows the "Saxy Kid," one of the people that some outsiders claimed was the last of the New River Shasta.

concluded that only one speaker remained. Since 1970, there have been many attempts to establish the family links between various native peoples and their Shasta roots. By 1989, people like Betty Hall, a Shasta historian, were publishing information that made it clear that the Shasta Nation had not disappeared. Today, the surviving Shasta people continue to struggle for the rights that they believe they are owed. The Shasta people are proud of their past and look to build a better future as both Native Americans and United States citizens.

Today, much of the Shasta region is popular with tourists. Here, visitors take in the sights of Mount Shasta, which last erupted in 1786.

Timeline

13,000–40,000 years ago	The ancestors of the Shasta people arrive in North America from Asia.
1540–1820	Europeans explore and begin to settle other parts of California. The Shasta people have no direct contact with the newcomers.
1820–1840	White trappers from Washington and Oregon make sporadic contact with the Shasta people.
1846–1848	The United States conquers California. The Shasta Nation now lives in a region claimed by the United States.
1849	The gold rush begins in the Sierra Nevada to the south of the Shasta territory. Miners soon arrive in the Mount Shasta area, searching for gold. They begin the destruction of the native communities and the theft of Shasta property.
1851	A treaty with the United States sets aside a part of Scott Valley for the Shasta people. It is not honored by the federal government.

1852	Fort Jones is established to the south of Mount Shasta to protect miners in northern California and southern Oregon. It will remain an important outpost until 1858.
1853	First Rogue River War. Fort Lane is established at the end of the conflict to protect miners. It will remain in operation until 1856.
1855–1856	Second Rogue River War. At the end of the conflict, surviving Shasta people are rounded up and forced to live at Grande Ronde and Siletz.
1863	Fort Klamath is founded by the United States in southern Oregon in part to control any Shasta who have escaped from the reservations. It remains an army post until 1889.
1870	Some Shasta people join the religious movement of Wavoka, who taught that special prayers and rituals could eliminate the newcomers.
1924	All Native Americans are made U.S. citizens.
1958	The two remaining Shasta reservations at Quartz Valley and Ruffeys are eliminated.
Today	The Shasta people continue their fight for recognition by the state and federal governments.

59

Glossary

alliance (uh-LY-uhnts) Close relationship formed between people or groups of people to reach a common goal.

archaeologist (ar-kee-AH-luh-jist) One who studies the remains and artifacts of past human life.

cranial deformation (KRAIN-ee-uhl deh-for-MAY-shun) A kind of change made to the skull that causes it to change its shape. The Shasta people practiced cranial deformation before the arrival of Europeans.

elder (EL-dur) One who is older.

epidemic (eh-pih-DEH-mik) Something, usually a disease, that affects a large number of individuals within a population or community.

glaciers (GLAY-shurz) Large masses of ice that move down a mountain or along a valley.

hopper mortar (HOP-pur MOR-tur) A special combination of basket, pestle, and stone slab that was used to grind acorns and similar foods into flour.

implements (IM-pluh-mentz) Tools or equipment.

leggings (LEH-gingz) Coverings for the legs.

legislature (LEH-jis-LAY-chur) A body of people that has the power to make or pass laws.

notorious (no-TOR-ee-us) Famous or well known, usually for something bad.

pestle (PEH-sul) A cylinder-shaped stone that is used with a mortar to grind nuts and seeds into flour.

sinew (SIN-yoo) A tendon.

Resources

BOOKS

Campbell, Paul D. *Survival Skills of Native Californians.* Salt Lake City: Gibbs Smith, 1999.

Malinowski, Sharon, ed. *Gale Encyclopedia of Native American Tribes.* Detroit: Gale Group, 1998.

Rawl, James J. *Indians of California: The Changing Image.* Norman, OK: University of Oklahoma Press, 1986.

MUSEUMS

Siskiyou County Museum
910 South Main Street
Yreka, CA 96097
(530) 842-3836
Web site: http://www.co.siskiyou.ca.us/museum/

WEB SITES

Due to the changing nature of Internet links, the Rosen Publishing Group, Inc., has developed an online list of Web sites related to the subject of this book. This site is updated regularly. Please use this link to access the list:

http://www.rosenlinks.com/lnac/shas

Index